Insects and Flowers

This book has been reviewed
for accuracy by
Walter L. Gojmerac
Professor of Entomology
University of Wisconsin—Madison.

Library of Congress Cataloging in Publication Data

Oda, Hidetomo.
  Insects and flowers.

  (Nature close-ups)
  Translation of: Hana to konchū / text by Hidetomo
Oda, photographs by Nanao Kikaku.
  Summary: Describes the relationship between insects
that eat plant nectar and the flowers that benefit
from their aid in pollination.
  1. Insect-plant relationships—Juvenile literature.
2. Pollination by insects—Juvenile literature.
[1. Insect-plant relationships. 2. Pollination]
I. Nanao Kikaku (Firm) II. Title. III. Series.
QL496.03513   1986   595.7'052482   85-28206
  ISBN 0-8172-2527-7 (lib. bdg.)
  ISBN 0-8172-2552-8 (softcover)

This edition first published in 1986 by Raintree Publishers Inc.

Text copyright © 1986 by Raintree Publishers Inc., translated from
Insects and Flowers copyright © 1976 by Jun Nanao and Hidetomo Oda.

Photographs copyright © 1976 by Nanao-Kikaku.

World English translation rights for *Color Photo Books on Nature*
arranged with Kaisei-Sha through Japan Foreign-Rights Center.

All rights reserved. No part of this book may be reproduced or utilized
in any form or by any means, electronic or mechanical, including
photocopying, recording, or by any information storage and retrieval
system, without permission in writing from the Publisher. Inquiries
should be addressed to Raintree Publishers Inc., 310 W. Wisconsin
Avenue, Milwaukee, Wisconsin 53203.

1 2 3 4 5 6 7 8 9 0   90 89 88 87 86

Insects and Flowers

Raintree Publishers
Milwaukee

▲ A white cabbage butterfly sipping nectar from the blossom of a rape plant.

On a warm midsummer day, the air is filled with the sound of insects humming and buzzing in a field of wildflowers. The sweet flower nectar provides food for many insects, such as butterflies and bees. And as it often happens in nature, the insects, in turn, do a service for the flowers. As they fly from plant to plant, sipping nectar, the insects carry tiny grains of plant pollen from one flower to another. Many plants need pollen from other blossoms in order to produce the fruits and seeds necessary to start new plants. The insects provide a way for this cross-pollination to take place.

▲ **A field full of rape blossoms.**

In some countries, rape is grown as cattle feed. In other countries, it is cultivated for the oil in its seeds.

◀ **The inside of a rape flower.**

The two lumps at the base of the leaves are the nectaries, which produce the sweet plant nectar.

▲ A hoverfly feeds on the pollen at the yellow center of this fleabane flower.

But plant pollination has not always been so efficient. Millions of years ago, insects didn't have wings. The plants on earth did not have flowers and had to depend on the wind to spread their seeds. But gradually, insects developed the ability to fly. And, over the centuries, plants developed bright and colorful flowers, their own scents, and the sweet tasting nectar that attracts insects.

However, there are still some non-flowering plants that rely on the wind to pollinate other plants. And sometimes, pollen is transferred from the male to the female organs on the same plant. That is called self-pollination.

▶ **A fleabane flower cut in half.**

The yellow part of the flower is made up of stamens, which are covered with male pollen grains.

▲ **A field of fleabane flowers.**

▲ A swallowtail butterfly sipping nectar from a morning glory.

Nectar, the sweet liquid secreted by plants, has a lot of sugar. It gives insects the energy they need to move about. Each type of insect has its own special way of gathering food.

Butterflies have a long, straw-like mouthpart called the proboscis. They use it for sucking nectar. When the proboscis is not in use, it is rolled up in a tight coil so it doesn't get in the butterfly's way. Bees have two stomachs. One of them, the crop, is used to carry nectar to the hive. Shield bugs, plant bugs, and other kinds of bugs have sucking mouthparts. They pierce plant stalks and suck the sap. Even mosquitoes feed on plant nectar most of the time. It is only the female mosquito that bites people. The human blood contains protein, which helps the eggs in her body to develop.

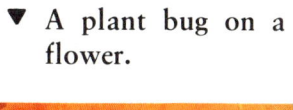

▲ These black ants have crawled inside a flower to lick its nectar.

▼ A small copper butterfly sucks the nectar from an inula flower.

▲ A honeybee pushing open the petals of a milk vetch flower.

◀ This shield bug has pollen on its long, needle-like proboscis.

▼ A plant bug on a flower.

▼ A mosquito sucks the nectar from an aster.

◀ A dronefly covered with pollen from a tulip.

◀ Fleabeetles eating the soft part of a sunflower before it has gone to seed.

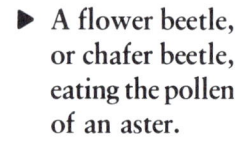

▶ A flower beetle, or chafer beetle, eating the pollen of an aster.

▶ A honeybee collecting pollen.

◀ A longhorned beetle eating nectar and pollen. A flower spider blends in with the yellow center of the flower.

◀ A hoverfly on a spiderwort flower.

▲ A hoverfly hovering at a spiderwort flower.

Plant pollen is rich in protein. It has the same value for bees and other insects that meat and eggs have for humans.

Insects have different ways of gathering the tiny, dust-like grains of pollen. Hoverflies have mouths as rough as sandpaper. They gather pollen and mash it into a kind of pulp. Honeybees have special hairs on their bodies for collecting pollen grains. Using their long legs, they brush the pollen from the underside of their abdomens, the back section of their body. Then they roll the pollen grains into a ball and carry it to the nest in special pollen baskets formed by their back legs.

▲ **A bee caught by a crab spider.**
Notice how the spider's color blends with the color of the flower, so that it is well-hidden.

▲ **A spider waiting for prey.**
A crab spider on an azalea waits for an insect to come near.

Not all insects eat plant nectar. Some are carnivorous, or meat-eaters. Dragonflies, praying mantises, and spiders are all hunters, or predators, of insects that sip plant nectar.

Many spiders trap insects in their webs. But the crab spider has a different way. Instead of spinning webs to catch their victims, crab spiders lie in wait for their prey on flowers and plants. When an insect comes along, the crab spider runs sideways, like a crab, and pounces on its victim. The spider bites the insect, paralyzing it. Then it sucks the body fluids.

With its long, green, stick-like body, the praying mantis stays hidden near a plant stem until an insect comes near. Then, with lightning speed, it reaches out with its front legs and grabs its victim.

▲ **A dryad butterfly caught by a praying mantis.**

The mantis moves very quickly to grasp its victim. The sharp claws on its front legs hold the butterfly tightly. It cannot escape.

▲ A ground-nesting bee crawls out of its nest.

Like other insects, ground-nesting bees gather pollen and nectar. But unlike honeybees and bumblebees, which live in colonies in hives, ground nesting bees are solitary creatures. Each female works all by herself to make a nest and stock it with food for her young.

The female bee tunnels into the earth to make her nest. Packing the dirt firmly to make the walls smooth, she forms many tiny, round cells. She makes one cell for each egg she lays. Then the bee sets out to stock the nest. She flies from flower to flower, collecting pollen and nectar.

▶ **The bee is an efficient eater.**

As it moves about on the flower petals, sipping nectar, tiny grains of pollen collect on the underside of the bee's body.

◀ **A bee drinking flower nectar.**

The bee uses its long tongue, with its spoon-like tip, to suck up flower nectar. It stores the nectar in its crop. When the bee is hungry, it lets some nectar pass from its crop to its stomach.

◀ A ground-nesting bee returns to her nest with a load of pollen.

▶ The inside of an underground nest.

A tiny ball of nectar and pollen, about the size of the tip of a matchstick, is placed in each cell. In the top cell, the tiny white bee egg rests on top of the ball of food.

When the bee returns to the nest with her precious cargo, she crawls underground. Then she regurgitates the nectar she has stored in her crop. She uses her long legs to scrape the pollen grains off her body. She mixes the pollen and nectar together and rolls it into a ball. Then the bee lays one long, thin, white egg on top of the ball of food in each cell. When the eggs hatch and the bee larvae emerge, they feed on the food in their nests. The young bees are able to grow by themselves without further care from the mother bee.

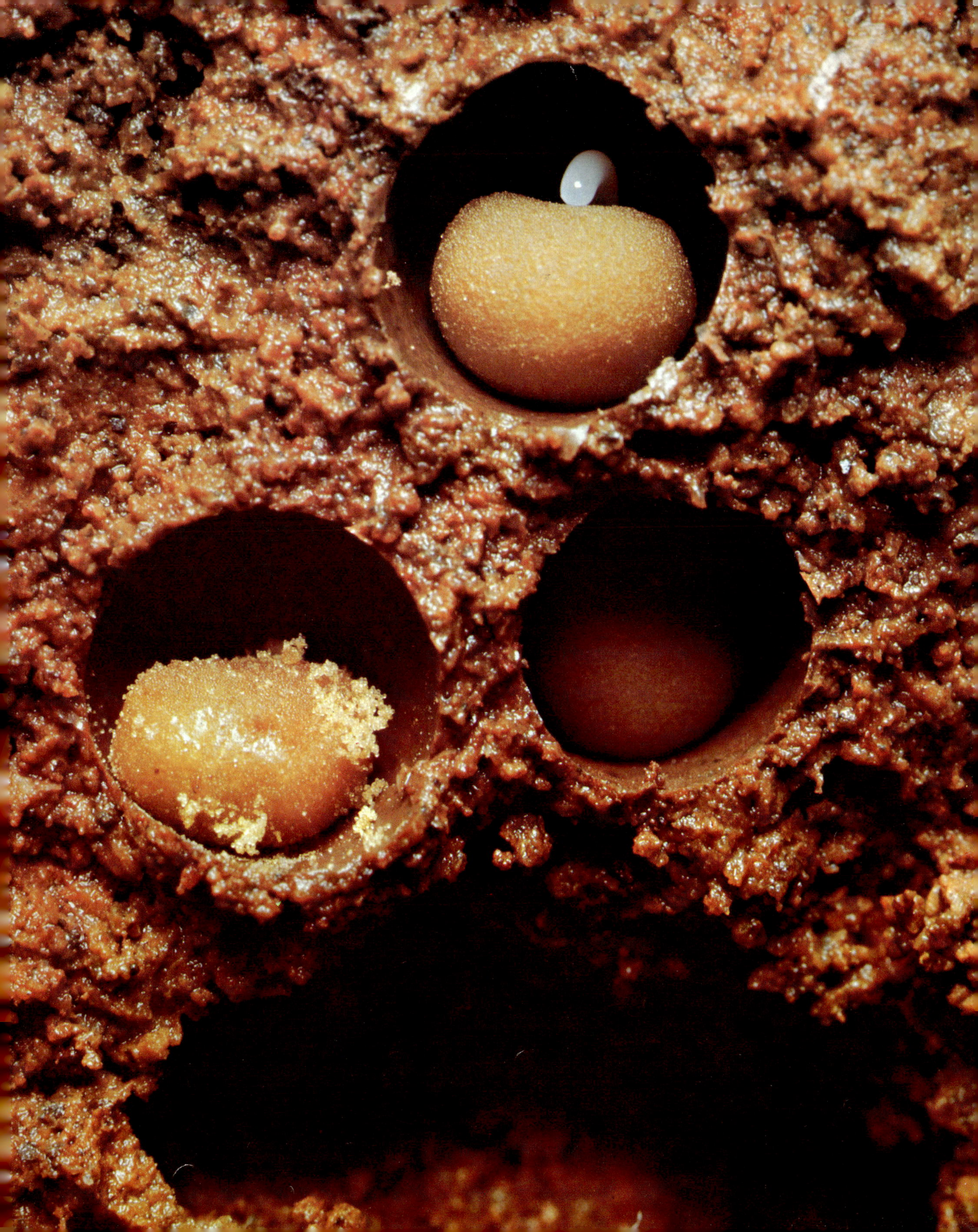

▲ A worker honeybee at a milk vetch plant.

▲ A honeybee sipping nectar from a thistle.

▲ A honeybee carrying pollen in its pollen baskets.

Unlike the ground-nesting bees, honeybees are social insects. Large colonies live together in hives. Each member of the colony has an important role to play in the bee community.

Each hive has one queen bee, dozens of male, or drone, bees, and thousands of worker bees. The queen bee's only purpose in life is to lay eggs. And she may lay a million of them in her lifetime. The drones do nothing but mate with the queen bee. It is the worker bees who build and maintain the nest, look after the queen bee, tend the young bee larvae, and gather food for the colony. Usually all the workers from a hive collect the nectar from only one kind of flower. In their short life spans, the worker bees visit hundreds of flowers in their search for food.

◀ **A honeybee's hive.**

This wooden hive was made for the bees by a beekeeper. Inside, the worker bees raise their young and build cells of wax in which honey is stored.

When a worker has discovered a good source of food, it returns to the hive to "tell" the other worker bees. The bee maps out the location of the flowers for the other workers by dancing. If the flowers are close by, the bee dances in a simple circle. If they are far away, the worker dances in a complicated figure-eight pattern. Scientists believe the complex dance points out the location of the flowers in relation to the sun. The slower the movement of the dancing bee, the greater the distance to the flowers.

With their long feelers, or antennae, the other worker bees pick up the scent of the flowers from the pollen carried by the dancing bee. Using the dance to tell the direction, the bees fly off in search of the new food source.

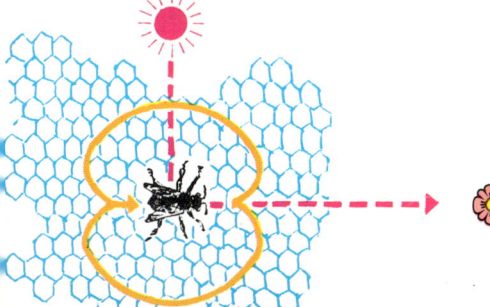

● **A honeybee performing a dance.**

From the way this bee dances, other bees know how to find the flowers. They also detect the scent of the flowers from the pollen the dancing bee is carrying.

▲ **A bee feeding other bees.**
The honeybee on the left regurgitates nectar from its crop and feeds other bees.

▲ **Workers feeding bee larvae.**
The young bee larvae are fed "beebread," a mixture of pollen and honey, by the worker bees.

Inside the nest there are thousands of tiny cells made of beeswax. When worker bees return to the hive with nectar, they regurgitate it from their crops and feed it to other bees in the hive. If the hive bees receive more nectar than they need, they store it in honey cells for future use. As moisture evaporates from the nectar, chemical changes take place and honey is formed. Later, the cells are capped with wax. During the winter, the bees eat the stores of honey. And that same honey is collected by beekeepers, sold in grocery stores, and eaten by people everywhere.

▲ **The cells inside a honeycomb.** The bee larva fills the bottom cell. Above it, a larva has become a pupa. The top cells are filled with pollen. The color of the pollen varies, depending on the kind of flower it comes from.

▲ A meadow of milk vetch.

◀ A bee sipping nectar from a milk vetch flower.

● A seed turns into a new shoot.

(1) The milk vetch dies, but the long tube-like female pistil is left. (2) After pollination takes place, the pistil swells up and looks like a pea pod. Inside, seeds form. (3) The pod dries up and bursts open. The seeds fall to the ground. (4) The seeds take root and later a new shoot appears.

The flowers on plants and trees provide insects with pollen and nectar. But the flowers also make seeds, which will grow into new plants. New milk vetch plants grow from vetch seeds, and dandelion plants grow from dandelion seeds.

In order for seeds to form and new flowers to grow, pollination must occur. Some flowers have both male and female cells and are capable of self-pollination. But seeds are more likely to grow when they are fertilized by pollen from another flower. So plants depend on insects, birds, or the wind to aid them in cross-pollination.

▶ If you looked at a milk vetch under a microscope, this is what the pistil would look like.

The tip of the pistil is called the stigma. The long narrow neck is the style. At the base is the ovary, where the eggs are located.

▶ **Surrounding the pistil of this milk vetch are ten long stamens with male pollen grains at their tips.**

The stamens are apart from the pistil so that it is more likely to be fertilized by pollen that an insect brings, rather than by the flower's own pollen.

Flowers are the reproductive parts of plants. Some flowers contain either male stamens or female pistils. Others, like this milk vetch plant, have both. Inside the petals of the milk vetch flower is a long thick tube, the pistil. The stigma, the tip of the pistil, is where pollen must touch in order for pollination to occur. When a pollen grain lands on the stigma, it absorbs water and sugar from the stigma and begins to swell up. Soon, it sends a narrow tube down the long neck, or style, of the pistil. When it reaches the base where the egg cells are, a sperm from the pollen joins with an egg. After the egg has been fertilized, a plant seed begins to grow.

▲ **The red spots on this azalea lead the hoverfly deep inside the flower.** Grains of pollen from the tips of the stamens are likely to stick to the fly's body as it walks by, searching for nectar.

▲ This bee pushes open the petals of an iris and disappears inside.

Over the centuries, flowers have developed bright colors, exotic markings, and strong perfumes, which attract insects to them. Flowers of particular colors attract certain kinds of insects. Because bees cannot see the color red, they are drawn to bright blue or yellow blooms. Snapdragons, clover, and columbines are all "bee" flowers.

Butterflies are attracted to orange or red flowers, which store their nectar deep inside the petals. With their long proboscises, butterflies can easily reach inside to drink the nectar. Some deep-throated flowers, like lilies, orchids, and azaleas, have colorful markings on their petals to guide insects far inside the flower to where nectar is stored.

◀ **The pale flowers of this evening primrose open at night.**

An elephant hawk moth sips the primrose nectar.

▶ **This touch-me-not is another night-blooming flower.**

A hummingbird hawk moth sips its nectar.

Insects that search for food during the day are attracted to flowers whose blossoms are open in daylight. But some insects, particularly moths, search for food at night. Night-blooming flowers, such as evening primroses and most kinds of orchids, open their blooms toward evening. These flowers are usually pale or white, colors which can easily be seen by insects at dusk. Often such flowers have heavy scents, which further attract insects to them.

And so, flowers and insects continue to help each other—in one of the most complex and mutually beneficial relationships in all of nature.

GLOSSARY

crop—a part of an insect's body used to store food. Both bees and ants have crops. (pp. 8, 15, 22)

cross-pollination—when pollen is transferred from one plant to another. (pp. 4, 25)

egg—a mature female germ cell. (p. 27)

fertilized—when an egg and a sperm unite, making it possible for a new organism to form. (p. 25)

ovary—the base of the pistil of a flower, where the eggs develop. (p. 26)

pistil—the female reproductive part of a plant. (pp. 25, 26)

pollen—the tiny grains that contain sperm cells which fertilize the plant's eggs. (pp. 4, 6, 11)

proboscis—an insect's tube-like mouth, which is used for sucking liquids. (pp. 8, 9, 29)

self-pollination—when pollen is transferred from the stamen to the pistil of the same plant (pp. 6, 25)

sperm—a mature male germ cell. (p. 27)

stamen—the male reproductive part of a plant. (pp. 6, 27)

stigma—the tip of a plant's pistil. (p. 27)

style—the long neck of a plant's pistil. (p. 27)